MW00935787

Fast Kids
Don't Train Slow

Fast Kids Don't Train Slow

The ultimate player's guide to running faster.

By **Dunte Hector** of ATX Speed

Published by **ATX Speed and Strength**
www.atxspeedandstrength.com
ISBN-13: 978-1974133475

This book was originally published in .MOBI format for Amazon Kindle.

This is an informative text about training for competitive ultimate by able-bodied athletes. No book can replace the experience of working with a professional face-to-face. The training programs in this book are meant to be self-contained, but take what works for you and discard the rest.

Use your own judgment when training. If something hurts, stop and see a professional. You are responsible for your choices and their consequences. None of the statements, suggestions, or ideas presented in this book are medical, financial, or legal advice of any sort.

We've done our best to provide accurate information, but the author encourages you to report errors and any other funny business you see in this book via email to dunte@atxspeedandstrength.com.

If you love what you read or if you wish it covered some other topic, please review the book on Amazon. Connect with the author at our website and sign up for the weekly *Speed & Strength Newsletter*.

Thanks for your investment in learning to run faster!

Resources & videos are available at
http://atxspeedandstrength.com/resources/FKDTS

Acknowledgments

This book would not have been possible without the critical eye and editing wizardry of Simon Pollock. He has cleaned up my ramblings about training since early 2016, first at Skyd Magazine and now at UltyResults. Simon, thank you for working on my ridiculous deadlines.

Melissa Witmer first invited me to the online magazine and graciously promotes my training ideas to her athletes. Thank you for giving me a platform to reach ultimate players around the world.

Ren Caldwell, Goose Helton, Stephen Hubbard, Tim Morrill, and Jonah Wisch -- thank you for sharing your ideas, for challenging my opinions, and for being professionals who relentlessly seek better training methods. You elevate my game.

Texas Showdown, Austin Sol, Cosa Nostra, Wildstyle, Moontower, Vortex, Melee, Tango, and the Beach Maedels of Germany -- thank you for trusting me and (sometimes) proving me right.

Dan John and Tony Holler -- I have absorbed so much of your wisdom over the years that many of these ideas are due to each of you.

For her patience with my writing schedule and for her edits to this book's early manuscript, I want to thank my wife Kate one million times over.

This book is dedicated to Sarah Levinn, an all-star player and Fast Kid with Texas Showdown.

You challenged me to share my training ideas with the entire ultimate community. Let's see how far my strong opinions can spread.

Table of contents

Chapter 1
Talking About Fast Kids

The Impact of Speed

In all sports, speed is king. In ultimate, particularly, people like to say, "You can't teach tall." When you listen to players describe what it takes to become great in this sport, it becomes evident that many believe you can't teach speed, either. We all know speed when we see it on the field: the defender that runs down his matchup, despite being three yards behind when the disc goes up; the cutter that gets separation on the first step, then catches a fifty yard huck with no one nearby; the short girl who is always mixing things up in the deep field when she appears from nowhere to knock down a disc.

Fast players are recognized for their special treasure, the ever-elusive quality of foot speed and masterful application of it on the field. Fans and competitors alike gaze at them in wonder, desperately wishing to have wheels for themselves. But athletes everywhere have either been force-fed or have willingly accepted that speed is not for them. Players seem unable to wonder how those on-field superstars *became* superstars and, thus, unable to fathom how they could become that, too.

Were They Born With It?

Listen to any interview with a world-class sprinter like Usain Bolt, Maurice Green, or Lolo Jones. It is simultaneously amazing and discouraging to hear them describe how they developed. Bolt, in particular, said this:

- "My parents were really great."
- "I played outside a lot."
- "Yes, I won all the races, even as a kid."

You might think, "Hey, I had great parents!"

Then you might think, "Oh, I was always playing outside, too!"
Then you will definitely think, "Crap, I did *not* win all the races."

Given only those three statements, knowing that you had the same environment and that you took the same actions but did not get the same results, it is natural to assume that you just don't have it.

Athletes believe fast folks are born with a special something. Players mournfully accept that, if they aren't the fast kid and have not always been the fast kid, they simply cannot drink from the fountain of speed. However, there are some details missing from the stories those world-class athletes tell.

Daniel Coyle in his bestseller The Talent Code was among the first widely published authors to crack open the jar on how the best *become* the best. He wrote one single sentence in that book that completely changed my coaching: "Historically, the gold and silver medalist in the 100 meters have been the second or third children in their families and had a talented, yet unremarkable older sibling."

Did you catch that? The interview with most champion sprinters should probably say:

- "My parents were really great."
- "I wanted to beat my older sister."
- "I played outside a lot."
- "Yes, I won all the races, even as a kid."

Coyle and Malcolm Gladwell became renowned with their speculation about the impact of 10,000 hours of practice being the path to excellence. Admittedly, committing 10,000 hours to anything is a daunting task. Many readers of either The Talent Code or Gladwell's Outliers readily accepted the authors' seemingly rational arguments: with enough practice, anyone could become world-class at the violin or on the tennis court.

But speed isn't a skill that you practice every day, with an established mechanical technique and standard method for practicing. Speed is still a mysterious million-dollar quality. And most of us just are not destined to become millionaires.

Right?

Don't Believe The Hype

With Peak, K. Anders Ericsson's tome on the development of expertise in any and every field, the jar was finally ripped open. Ericsson's research informed Coyle's theory about the development of physical skills and it inspired Gladwell's theory of the factors contributing to huge success. In a way, Peak is the story beneath the story.

In it, Ericsson makes a bold claim: with early support, frequent playful competition, strong desire to improve, and a bit of obsession to see through the rigorous boredom of daily practice, absolutely anyone can and will achieve excellence in *any* skill, whether physical, mental, or otherwise.

In A Kind of Grace, Jackie Joyner-Kersee provided more depth about her development, saying, "I have always hated losing," "my older brother's friends were my friends, too, and I wanted to do what they did," and "I won my first race in middle school."[1]

Maybe you're already seeing the pieces. Conversations with the world's fastest humans have unearthed several factors that may help dispel the myths about speed:

- Supportive parents
- Older sibling after whom to model
- Daily competition with older, stronger, faster kids
- Vigorous, frequent play
- Resentment of losing
- Strong desire to improve or catch up
- 10-12 years of growth and development

Peak brought all the ideas together about becoming the best. With his explorations of a variety of sport performers in addition to great thinkers, great musicians, and great everybody elses, Erics-

---

[1] Jackie's brother Al Joyner was anything *but* unremarkable, as the 1984 Olympic gold medalist in the triple jump, though Jackie's 6 Olympic medals casts a long shadow...

son offered definitive proof that the special something about speed might just be in your head.

Believe You Can Be Faster

The most critical skill of speed, more important than what I know about training and running fast, more important than what the experts can tell us about becoming the best, and far more important than what your peers will tell you, is what you believe. If you believe speed is a genetic gift, a sip from the magical fountain before birth that cannot be attained later in life, then this book cannot help you.

But if you believe that speed is a skill, one you could develop and master given the guidance and enough time, and if you desperately want it for yourself and are willing to strive, to strain, and to suffer for it, then I wrote this book to show you the path.

In it, you will find the how, the what, the when, and the where of becoming faster. The why? To run down more hucks, to get more Ds, to need less endurance because no one can run with you long enough to make you tired. To get open more often, more easily, and more consistently. To be the all-star on your team who everyone can rely on to chase errant throws and make the game-saving catch.

The who of speed? That's *YOU*.

What This Book Is Not

But I have two final warnings.

First, this book can't do everything for you. When experts in any field are interviewed, they describe their work as their craft. Experts produce huge volumes of consistently high-quality work. The best writers have a half-dozen bestselling books to their names; the best musicians have multiple Grammy nominations; the best golfers are at every professional tournament; the best sprinters have an enviable collection of gold medals.

Your craft is playing ultimate. And, for the most part, you have to maintain that focus on being the best ultimate player you can be. This book cannot improve your throwing, cannot improve the timing of your cuts, and cannot improve your on-field tactics. Though this book can show you how to become faster and becoming faster can make you a more dominant force on the field, no all-star is a one-dimensional speed demon.

All-stars make smart throws, clear hard to make space, and get wide open in useful field positions. All-stars are supportive teammates, invest time and energy in deeply knowing the playbook, and hold themselves accountable. This book *cannot* make you an all-star if you blindly pursue speed and neglect the dozen other skills it takes to play this game.

Keep in mind, in my time training ultimate players, I have researched and analyzed the specific conditioning this sport requires. Since you are a smart player who is committed to improving your game, *Chapter 5* has your in-season conditioning needs covered. But you still need skill practice!

Second, this book can't make you faster quickly. There are no six-week solutions to speed. If you've chosen this book, you likely feel you aren't fast enough. You will make noticeable progress in your first two months following the training programs presented here. But progress in speed, like anything else, is *not linear*. If you do everything right 100% of the time, sticking faithfully to the plan and designing your entire life around the training necessary to become faster, you will still have ruts and plateaus in your on-field improvements. There are more factors to running faster than just moving your legs quickly. The training programs in this book will improve those factors individually and integrate them into a coherent, graceful, blazing-fast whole...but they don't all improve at the same rate.

Given just eight weeks on this program, you *will* be faster on the track and during play. But eight weeks barely captures the low-hanging fruit. Because of the season and its impact on your body, there are only six months each year available for true speed training. Remember that elite sprinters had committed 10-12 years of skill-developing practice to their craft *before* they committed 10 years to becoming the best they could possibly be.

I'm not asking for 10 years, but I ask that you give this book an honest two seasons of training. That would be one full training year, all together, and at the end of it, you will be astonished at the progress you've made. There are no six-week solutions to speed. The fountain of speed is bountiful and anyone can drink from it, but like the Fountain of Youth, you have to endure a long journey to find it.

In order to grasp the special something of becoming faster, it helps to first understand what speed is not. That's up next.

Chapter 2:
Analyzing Fast Kids

What is Speed?

We are going on a journey toward speed together. You should be certain the path we are following leads where you want to go. Stop reading for a moment to answer this question: *What, exactly, is speed to you?*

In my early days working with Texas ultimate players, I asked every athlete what they hoped to accomplish. Five different athletes would offer five different descriptions of the speed they wanted to improve.

- "cut harder"
- "get open downfield"
- "first step"
- "coming from behind to make a D"
- "creating space early"

You probably know exactly in what situations on the field you get smoked. You probably remember the disappointment of watching a cutter run away from you after 15 yards. You probably still feel the frustration of a defender coming from behind to knock down your disc. Keep those feelings. You will need them when it is time to train. For now, though, accept the basic purpose of speed development:

Speed development improves your absolute highest running speed.

For every athlete at every level, there are three phases to running all out. First, you accelerate from either standing still or jogging. Second, you move as fast as you can. Third, you get tired and slow down.

How well you accelerate is critical to every ultimate player, but training for acceleration is not speed development. Because the two phases cannot be separated, acceleration will also improve when the second phase improves. If you only train acceleration using hill sprints and sleds, however, top speed may not improve.

Success at top speed is measured in miles per hour (mph)[2]. You can count yourself in the upper ranks when you run over 17 mph as a woman or 20 mph as a man.[3] A table is provided in the training section for monitoring your progress and converting running speed to different units.

In ultimate, few players encounter the third phase during play. Deep cutters and their defenders only occasionally go 60+ yards from a standing start in a completely straight line. They can get some benefit from running long sprints and building up speed endurance. Most players, however, will never use that speed endurance in a game. This is the first misconception to be cleared up about speed.

Speed Is Not Endurance

I have been ruffling feathers about training for ultimate since 2015. Traditional ideas about training for ultimate involve jogging, interval runs, sprint repeats, and elaborate agility sessions. Within strength and conditioning, a lot of coaches think sports-specific training is the key to success and that weight room skills equate to athletic performance.

Athletes at ATX Speed and Strength train the highest return-on-investment qualities like speed, single-leg strength, and mental preparation, then ignore most other qualities completely. At best, other qualities are a distraction. At worst, they are damaging to your health and longevity. If you have been in the game for a while, get your feathers ready:

---

[2] Generally, measurements are offered in Imperial units for my American readers. For the most part, consider yards equivalent to meters (60 yards ~ 60 meters). When necessary for measurement, exact conversions are presented in these footnotes.

[3] But you will never be too fast!

"Track workouts" are a waste of time and probably cause more injuries than layouts or rough game fields.

Two or three players on the field might take two or three legitimate full-speed 60+ yard runs in a game. Out of two 17-player rosters, up to 9% of players *might* need sprinting ability over long distances. They **might** need the endurance to do this eight times in one day in the most competitive tournaments in fair weather. Factor in unfavorable winds, reliable handlers that can slowly work a disc down the field, or consistent flow in the deep field, and the wildest O-line and D-line cutters will take five long sprints per competition day.

The odds are against needing the ability to sprint long and the only players doing so are already the fastest on the team. What good is having your entire squad slog through five, ten, or twenty painful 200-meter runs every week at practice?

Imagine a player named Anne running 200-meter repeats on a Tuesday. Anne feels awesome on rep number one. Her teammates are all fired up, the music is pumping from the portable stereo, and Anne feels like proving something. She runs the first rep in 28 seconds.

After the second rep, run in 29.5 seconds, Anne's legs are feeling heavy. Her quads and calves are burning and her heart is racing. Everything is moving according to plan.

Anne eases off in the fourth rep about 10 yards before the finish line and runs 32 seconds. Her whole body shivers. She stumbles while she tries to regain her breath and her head feels cloudy. Her captain is calling for everyone to hurry back to the start line, but Anne is lurching across the field, fighting for air, and shaking stars out of her eyes.

Anne is the team's star handler, who typically receives the dump and puts the disc through a narrow lane for consistent 10-15 yard gains. The fifth 200-meter run is likely to be slower and more painful… how does this session help Anne make explosive first steps, efficient five-yard accelerations, or throw under pressure? On the occasion Anne has to cut hard or bid for a poorly thrown disc, how will this session help her accelerate, turn, or jump?

When your muscles burn from the waste products of anaerobic glycolysis[4], they stop functioning well. There are cramps or spasms and you feel nauseated. Your eyes get foggy, your head pounds, and your speech slurs. Because of all this stress to your body, your sprint technique gets worse with every rep you run. As your running technique gets worse and you run slower, every rep looks and feels *less* like the intense burst-and-recover of ultimate. Every slow, painful step pounds your feet, shins, knees, hips, and lower back. And none of it contributes directly to your ultimate game.

Anne, the handler, is hurting her game with track workouts. To the cutter who actually needs speed endurance, they are *losing* the ability to make incredible 60+ yard dashes downfield to catch big hucks because they are never practicing the ability to run *fast* under fatigue. If your best cutter took the first 200-meter run in 26 and the fifth in 31, which is impressive endurance, they are still running 20% **slower** by the fifth rep! Many crucial games are won on hucks into the endzone. It seems unwise to bet your victory on finishing your training sessions at 80% of your best for three months.

The fastest player wins after the first pull and the fastest player still wins on universe point. Speed is not endurance. Track workouts don't make you faster.

Speed Is Not Strength

Many ultimate players either intuitively or habitually avoid weight training. From the perspectives of injury prevention or reaping easy

---

[4] Anaerobic glycolysis is burning sugar without air, a process which creates acidic waste

gains in jumping ability, this is a mistake. That will have to be explored in another book. In at least one way, however, players are right to do this.

As ultimate grows, players will hire personal trainers and strength & conditioning coaches. Many will be disappointed with the results from that investment. Trainers and coaches often believe the stronger a player is, the faster they are.

The easiest way for a coach to get you stronger is to increase your muscular bodyweight. The fastest way to run slower is to gain significant bodyweight. Since many professionals do not really believe speed can be improved (and few would admit this), the conflict of objectives should be evident.

The company Bigger Faster Stronger has been a trendsetter in football strength & conditioning since 1976. As the name implies, they put a premium on bigger players lifting more weight in the weight room. Unfortunately, they only pay lip service to speed development. Worse, when trainers and coaches think of making athletes stronger and faster for sports, they default to the same training methods Bigger Faster Stronger promotes.

Outside of college and professional sports, most of what passes for strength training is simply lifting weights. Despite my background in the strength sports and my zeal for weight training, I want to be clear: Lifting weights won't make you faster.

Do you like to lift light weights for many repetitions at a slow, controlled tempo, believing the steady output will improve your endurance? Ultimate is not a continuous endurance sport and speed is the polar opposite of light, slow, or controlled.[5]

Do you like to lift heavy weights for a few repetitions explosively, believing the large loads will improve your power and jumping

---

[5] Light weights for many repetitions are not even helpful in endurance sports! Might need another book for that one.

ability? Ultimate occasionally rewards big vertical jumps from a standstill, but the two-legged build-up of force that big weights require still does not translate to running fast.[6]

Do you like to lift medium weights for many repetitions and feel your muscles pump with blood, believing the burn is a sign of gains? Ultimate punishes muscle mass gain. That training method is perfect for gaining mass. A heavier object is harder to accelerate, quicker to fatigue, and lands harder against the ground. You do not want to be a heavier object.

Your ability to accelerate -- phase one of every running cycle -- determines the top speed -- phase two -- that you can reach. Bigger muscles make heavier bodies. Heavier bodies have weaker acceleration and lower top speeds. That adds up to slower athletes.

Read that again:
Bigger muscles = slower athletes.

But legions of personal trainers and strength & conditioning[7] coaches equate bigger with stronger and stronger with faster. Be wary of any expert telling you to lift weights in order to become faster. Guard your time and your money. Muscle mass is not strength. Speed is not strength. Lifting weights won't make you faster.

Speed Is Electricity

People believe athletes are just born with that special something for a simple, though misguided, reason. All of us tend to either doubt or place blind faith in what we cannot see. And we cannot see what creates speed.

---

[6] I cannot improve on what Joel Smith's <u>Vertical Foundations</u> and <u>Vertical Ignition</u> books have said about training to jump higher. Read them.

[7] Did you notice that *strength & conditioning* contains no reference to speed? There are some great S&C coaches out there who understand speed...but there are far more meatheads.

But research and experience are catching up. Peter Weyand observed that the fastest runners place the greatest vertical forces into the ground with each footstrike. Frans Bosch observed that the fastest runners achieve the same body positions at top speed, almost without regard to height, limb length, or gender.

Sprinters observed that the best exercises for running fast *feel like* running fast. Archie Hahn and Charlie Paddock noticed in the early 20th century that bounding felt like the foot contact of sprinting; Nikolay Ozolin noticed in the late 20th century that depth drops felt like the impact of sprinting; track & field coaches throughout history noticed that hurdle hops felt like the timing of sprinting.

The components of great sprinting are hard to see, yet easy to feel. Personal trainers and strength & conditioning coaches do not mislead you in your quest for speed out of malice. Most coaches outside of track & field are slow. They cannot see what makes people fast and have never felt it for themselves.

In the 1800s, the outspoken critics of Thomas Edison and Nikola Tesla did not put down those pioneers' claims solely to discourage them. The critics had never experienced electricity. They could not see how current flowed and had never felt it for themselves.

Speed is electricity.

Until you experience speed, you cannot understand what it is.

After your first two or three steps, the actions of running fast are mostly reflexive. The human nervous system, which is a superhighway of electrical connections from your brain to your body's tissues, can transmit signals as fast as 266 mph[8]. According to neuroscience research, reflexes, also controlled by electrical connections, are *at least* twice as fast.

---

[8] 119 meters per second!

When your body is placed into correct positions, the actions of running fast occur faster than conscious control. When something is too fast to think, it is much too fast to see.

Reflexes operate with a ripple effect. A stretch reflex occurs at your big toe as your foot hits the ground. This causes tissues in the sole of your foot to pull on your Achilles and calf, which pull on your hamstrings and hip muscles. The stretch occurring at your hip pulls on the opposite shoulder and, because that tension crosses your body, there is also a stretch in your stomach and back muscles.[9]

Remember that this occurred because your big toe hit the ground. The ripple effect causes both a stretch *and* a contraction before your big toe leaves the ground. In slow people, that means force moves from your toe to the top of your head and back in *fifteen hundredths of a second*, 0.15 seconds. In fast people, the entire action set of running fast occurs in *one tenth of a second*, 0.10 seconds. In very fast people, the entire action set of running fast occurs in *eight hundredths of a second*, 0.08 seconds.

It can be easy to dismiss these numbers. You might be thinking, "Point-one-five isn't so different than point-zero-eight!" Look again:

- 0.15 seconds = 150% of 0.10 seconds
  Slow people are on the ground **50% longer** than fast people.
- 0.15 seconds = 188% of 0.08 seconds
  Slow people are on the ground **88% longer** than *very* fast people!

I know that percentages can be overwhelming. Think of it this way: when a tortoise races a hare, every two tortoise steps is three hare steps. And when a tortoise races a greyhound, every two tortoise steps is four greyhound steps.

---

[9] The very first time you really run fast, you will be sore in strange places the next day.

No matter what the tortoise sees or thinks he sees, he cannot possibly understand what makes the hare and greyhound run so fast.

Slow coaches who do not study speed cannot possibly understand what it would feel like to be nearly twice as effective with every step. When something is too fast to understand, it is far too fast to see.

Speed is not endurance.
Speed is not strength.
Speed is electricity.

Track workouts will not make you faster. Lifting weights will not make you faster. But practicing running in a way that maximizes electrical signals and reflex actions will increase the speed at which your body transmits those electrical signals and the effectiveness of those reflex actions.

Remember Anne, our all-star handler wasting her talent on 200-meter repeats? The good news for her is that the reflexes which control absolute maximum speed also control all other running-related reflexes. That means improving top speed will improve acceleration, ability to stop, and ability to jump off one leg. Top speed is the master quality for all fast movements.

Speed is a skill. Like any skill, it can be improved.

As Illinois high school track coach Anthony Holler says, "Speed grows like a tree." There are a few weeks of exciting growth; quiet weeks and months as the roots expand outward; quieter months and years of slow, but steady progress as the tree gains its rings. Now that you know what speed is and what it is not, let's plant your tree.

Chapter 3:
Characteristics of Fast Kids

Speed Development is Simple

The path ahead is not as hard as it seems. You have already made a similar commitment. You have grown as an ultimate player by hundreds of hours practicing and refining your throwing, catching, and marking.

You have it in you. Choose speed.

You will be glad you did.

I wish speed were more complicated. I wish I had the audacity to make it seem complicated. If either were the case, I could make a lot of money teaching speed. Running faster, like having pristine heart health or six-pack abs, is difficult to sell honestly. What do running fast, cardiovascular health, and visible abdominal muscles have in common?

All of those goals require consistent, disciplined adherence to simple, mind-numbingly boring principles.

> To have six-pack abs eat a controlled diet every day…
> To have a healthy heart exercise moderately every week…
> To run fast practice running fast every training day…
> *…for several years in a row.*

That kind of consistency, discipline, and faith to show up, day after day, week after week, month after month, year after year is simple hard work.

So if you really want to plant a tree and grow speed, read on. If you will not commit to hundreds of hours practicing and refining the same skills, give up on running faster right now.

You can have the burn of sprint repeats, the pump of bodybuilding weights, and the aching lungs of being winded at the end of every point trying to catch the fast kids… or you can invest your time and energy into *becoming* one of the fast kids.

Your choice.

Speed is simple and I want to deliver that simplicity, well, simply. Becoming faster requires only three things:

1. "good enough" technique
2. frequent, intense competition
3. consistent rest & recovery

The Seeds of Speed

There is a right way to do everything. A right way to throw a flick in a crosswind; a right way to mark when forcing backhand from the sideline; a right way to clear when cutting. Ultimate players have determined the right way to execute on the field from years of competing, strategizing, sharing ideas, and experimenting. You have learned, and continue to learn with every rep, that these skills are more difficult than they seem.

The trouble with speed is that it looks so *easy*! Every sprinter in an Olympic 100-meter final looks more or less the same. No one seems to be working very hard. Fast defenders at Nationals move their feet fast and catch up to receivers. It just doesn't look complicated.

Remember, though, speed is electricity. Our eyes deceive us.

Correct technique is the seed of speed. Few athletes are taught to run. Fewer still are taught to run fast. Some coaches believe there is no reason to teach athletes how to run, arguing that running is an instinct-driven gross motor pattern. There is some truth to that argument. If you watch elementary school-age children race, many of them make it to the finish line without a catastrophic wipeout. But to watch a random 1st grader run against a trained 1st grader in a race on the track is to notice several ways that focused kid winning by 15 yards is different.

There is an optimal technique for sprinting and it is an absolute necessity when success in your sport completely depends on being faster than everyone else in a competition. Speed is important. It is the master physical quality for any athlete who runs. But remember the warning in Chapter 1. You are a competitive ultimate player who wants to run fast, not a sprinter who plays ultimate for fun. You need to be faster than other ultimate players, not faster than all the other fast humans.

So we should emphasize good enough or sufficient technique for sprinting, when the goal is becoming a faster ultimate player. That is simple to attain. Don't let your eyes fool you.

Simple does not mean easy.

The Hard Z Position

This position, what I call the Hard Z, is the Rosetta Stone of sprinting. It is the lens through which all other running actions, all training objectives, and all practice sessions can be analyzed.

The Hard Z Position

In the Hard Z, these features are key:

- head to ankle bone, your body forms a rigid, straight line
- your support ankle is flexed, meaning your toes are moving away from your shin
- your swinging knee rises to the height of your hip bone
- your swinging ankle is cocked, meaning your toes are pulled up to your shin
- your arms move opposite to your legs and at similar angles

During technique practices, the Hard Z can be summed up as "stand tall, knee up, toe up."

The key to running fast is hidden in this position. This position is Speed Technique #1. There is no Speed Technique #2.

In the Design Posture training program, most of the awkward and silly postures you have to hold reinforce the Hard Z. Drills to support that position show up in every warmup, in every strength session, and in every running rep. The Hard Z is important to understand and to master, so you will get to practice it daily.

Speed refers to the fastest you can move your body through space. The Hard Z, being a static position, does not completely define what it takes to run fast. Nearly any athlete, whether completely untrained in running or beaten down by 200-meter repeats, can attain the Hard Z position when standing still. Your challenge is "striking a pose" while moving fast. The athlete who can hit the Hard Z position repeatedly, consistently, and when fatigued is likely to also be the fastest athlete on the field.

You should ask why!

Because the qualities which make it possible to hit the Hard Z posture correctly and quickly are exactly the qualities required to run fast.

Ankles, knees, & hips

Physically, all you need to improve in order to run faster are your ankles, your knees, and your hips. If you have explosive muscles around your ankle joint, your feet can absorb the impact of hitting the ground and initiate the stretch reflex ripple effect. If you have explosive muscles around your knee joint, your legs can accept the impact of hitting the ground and return it 100%. If you have explosive muscles around your hips, your thigh can be placed in the correct position to react to the impact of the ground efficiently.

The biomechanics of sprinting get pretty complicated.

Just remember this: if the muscles around your ankle bone, knee, and hips are all trained well, you can hit the Hard Z at high speed and that is how you run faster.

We can distill the two qualities you are trying to build to these: *stiff ankles* and *the hip lock*.

Stiff ankles

The ankle is a joint, which is the meeting point of two or more bones. A joint cannot inherently be stiff. The tissues which connect those bones, however, can and there are two kinds of stiffness.

The first kind of stiffness, what you probably imagine when you read "stiff," is inflexible or stuck. The first kind of stiffness describes how your joints feel after the nine-hour flight to Windmill or how your shoulders feel after carpooling home from Nationals with your six smelliest friends.

The second kind of stiffness, what track coaches mean when they say elastic power, is quick to react and without sag. The second kind of stiffness describes a seamless interaction between muscles and tendons that keeps a joint locked in position while tissues absorb huge forces then rebound those forces to propel you forward.

Watch any slow-motion video[10] of an elite sprinter's ankle after leaving the blocks. His foot will look frozen in space when his toes strike the track. Then his body rockets forward and his toes roll off the ground moments later, without the heel moving backward at all. It looks so easy!

But for that "frozen" ankle to support a 200 pound human accelerating from 0 miles per hour to 10 miles per hour[11] in one step and for that ankle to not sag or bend at all so every unit of energy he produces can be transmitted to the ground is remarkable indeed. The efficiency and explosiveness of calf and foot muscles which make this possible are what track coaches mean by stiff ankles.

Whether in acceleration or while running at top speed, the stiffness of your ankle determines your running economy. A stiff ankle not only means no energy from your butt and legs is wasted; it means energy created by reflexes can be used for running, too. Reflex energy is nearly free. If you keep joints stiff during every stride, you will not only run faster, but at lower energy cost. In ultimate, that means you can run faster more often before you get tired.

Fast people have stiff ankles. It takes them less energy to run. So fast people stay fast for longer in any given game.

Hip lock

If you have ever searched the Internet for relief from back pain caused by a desk job, you've probably come across discussions of pelvic position. Many solutions to back pain describe your pelvis as a bowl and short, tight hip flexors as a primary source of your pain. By holding your bowl in a neutral position, so none of its imagi-

---

[10] David Oliver acceleration video: https://youtu.be/wEufQI-hHjQ?t=30s
[11] 91kg man accelerating from 0 m/s to 4.5 m/s

nary water spills while you walk, you gradually lengthen and relax your hip flexors, alleviating pain. That is good advice. We could all stand to improve our posture and pelvic position.

For athletic performance, however, the "neutral bowl" pelvis is an incomplete model. It really only applies when viewing a body from the side while walking. At high speed, things change. Without digging too deep into topics the Gait Guys[12] cover better anyway, here's what matters most: your bowl *should be neutral* front-to-back pretty much all the time. But in order to run fast, your bowl *must not be neutral* left-to-right!

Look at these athletes during their stance phase of a running stride, which is when the body is fully supported on one leg. Whether changing direction, accelerating, or running at top speed, their bowl *tips to one side*. If that's all you take from this, however, you are letting your eyes fool you again. It looks so easy.

Stance phase while changing direction.

---

[12] YouTube @theGaitGuys, biomechanics & rehab for athletic feet.

Stance phase during early acceleration.

Late stance phase at high speed.

The key element of a hip lock is that, when in the stance phase on your right leg, your right hip is fixed in space and your left hip is *pushed upward explosively*. Look at this athlete during the stance phase. This is not sprinting. This is slow running. Take his bent knee and flat foot as evidence: this is ***hip drop***, rather than hip lock.

Hip *drop* during stance phase of a sprint finish.

The hip lock is inseparable from the Hard Z position. Your support leg during the stance phase has to be nearly straight; your support ankle must be stiff and slightly flexed.

Stiff ankles + hip lock = FAST

When all the pieces come together, you strike the Hard Z while moving fast. When you achieve the Hard Z while moving fast, each step either preserves your precious momentum or increases your running speed, depending on the phase of running you are in. Achieving the Hard Z requires stiff ankles, so no energy is lost to a squishy ankle joint during acceleration. Achieving the Hard Z requires the ability to hip lock, so no energy is lost to a bent knee or soft butt during each stride.

Standing tall on one leg isn't very hard. Lifting your knee isn't very hard. Lifting your toes isn't very hard. Achieving the Hard Z looks so easy. But standing still is not running fast, no matter how good you look doing it.

Once your body is strong enough and stiff enough to achieve these positions, achieving the Hard Z can no longer be done consciously. By building stiff ankles and a strong butt, you've met the minimum requirements for running fast. Everything else has to be left to electricity -- reflexes and coordination.

This book won't attempt to explore the elastic tissue behaviors and neuromuscular signaling that have to occur in order to run really fast. Frans Bosch's <u>Running</u> does a brilliant job.[13]

That's the whole thing about speed technique. Master the Hard Z by building stiff ankles and perfecting the hip lock and you will have the physical qualities to run fast. Technique is the seed from which your speed tree will grow. But where to plant it?

The Soil of Speed

Remember our interviews with elite sprinters from Chapter 1? Usain Bolt described his circumstances best in his autobiography <u>Faster Than Lightning</u>: he was an energetic kid who played outside every day with older kids and he hated to lose. The first race he ever won involved a box lunch for the winner and an empty stomach for the loser. In chapter 1, it was demonstrated that elite sprinters, even early on, hated losing so much that they ran fast in order to avoid it.

If you play ultimate competitively, you probably hate to lose. Good news! The best environment for speed is one in which you are des-

---

[13] With any of Bosch's books, be prepared for a heavy, nerdy text on how humans run fast.

perate to avoid losing. The soil of speed is frequent, intense competition.

Slow coaches complain that sprinters are lazy. They think sprinters won't work hard. Slow coaches' concept of hard work is interval runs, long jogs, and punishing exercise circuits. When sprinters don't give 100% during this "hard work," coaches say those athletes are not motivated.

Slow coaches don't understand just how hard it is to run fast.

Fast athletes aren't lazy and they aren't unmotivated. Fast athletes are extremely motivated. When the stakes are high, fast athletes have a reputation to uphold and an ego to feed. If you're hungry to be one of the fast athletes, you will have to embrace this mentality: everything is a competition and it's always a race.[14]

There are three ways to introduce competition to your speed training that are surprisingly simple. In exchange for brevity, remember this: every single rep you ever run in a speed training session should occur in one of these three competitive contexts. Any rep you run that is NOT in one of these competitive contexts is NOT going to make you faster.

Context 1: run down a disc.

Have a friend huck a disc 30+ yards. As the disc leaves their fingers, you accelerate from a standing start, rise to top speed, and fight with all you have to catch the disc.[15] If your friend has great touch, they should try to put the disc straight down the lane and should send it 5 more yards every time you are successful.

---

[14] I have learned over the years that ultimate players will compete in anything and everything, so this shouldn't be a difficult mental switch.

[15] C'mon, you know what this looks like.

Context 2: run down an opponent.

Be a practice hero, but intentionally handicap yourself. With another friend throwing hucks, deliberately let your opponent get 2-3 steps on you after the disc, then chase them down, attempting to get a block without laying out. The psychology of swatting down a disc as you blow past a receiver keeps you honest and creates intensity when you train.

Context 3: time your sprints.

Use a stopwatch or electronic timing equipment to objectively measure every rep you run. Chase times. Faster is always better.

If you are training by yourself on an open field, there is no accountability for actually giving 100% effort. You could be moving pretty fast but only be running at 90%. Submaximal (less than all-out) running is not speed training. So either get a disc to chase, a friend to chase, or times to chase. Slow coaches don't understand this, but sprinters know it is hard work. Competition is the soil of speed. But how to keep your tree growing?

The Nourishment of Speed

Big cats sleep more than 20 hours per day. Rabbits and housecats and your German Shepherd Samson take dozens of short naps, too. In every animal for which running fast is a priority, sleep is a prized activity.

Take a lesson from this: power loves rest.

Bodybuilding magazines and articles about strength training offer long essays about protein intake, amino acids, frequent small meals, supplements, and water intake. Often there is a footnote or two about getting enough sleep. If you want to build up your muscles, planning meals and nutrient timing might be as important as sleep.

But if you want to build up your speed and the electrical circuits which control it, food is almost irrelevant and sleep is everything. Up next is a short lesson on why.

Quick Lesson:
Muscle Adaptation vs Brain Adaptation

There are two major theories about human adaptation: Selye's Theory of the General Adaptation Syndrome for muscle cells and neuroscience's Theory of Myelination for neurons.

According to Selye's General Adaptation theory, stress is applied to the cell, which causes the cell's functions to slow. This is the alarm phase. When the stress ends, the cell uses your body's resources for repair. Repairs continue until the cell's capacity for stress is slightly greater than the original stress applied. This is the resistance phase. Finally, if stress is applied too frequently or too intensely, the cell dies or is inhibited from further adaptation. This is the exhaustion phase.

When Handler Anne ran 32 seconds on her fourth 200-meter repeat and it made her head swirl, this was the alarm phase. If Anne had stopped after the fourth rep, then repeated that session a few days later, she would find that her fourth rep either hurt less in the same 32 seconds or could be run in 31.5 seconds with the same amount of pain. That would be the resistance phase. But her fifth rep that Tuesday, her intention to run *six* reps next Tuesday, and her efforts to add more slow reps every week are a shortcut to the exhaustion phase.

When your goal is muscle mass or endurance, the improvement you want lies within muscles. General Adaptation Syndrome describes how your muscles adapt to training. But when your goal is coordination, the improvement you want is electric and involves precisely timing the actions of different body parts. The Theory of Myelination describes how your brain adapts to training.

In Chapter 2, you learned that your nervous system is a superhighway of brain-to-muscle connections. Each connection looks like a thin copper wire that stretches either from your brain out to a given muscle (long-cycle connection) or directly from your spinal cord to a muscle (reflex connection). Those wires are nerves. Like the copper wires in precision electrical systems, your nerves are insulated. A thin sleeve of jelly, called myelin, does for your nerves what rubber does for copper wire: protects the nerve from damage and allows faster transmission of signals.

According to the Theory of Myelination, every time you practice a skill, your brain adds a little jelly to your nerve wire while you sleep. The more you practice a skill and get quality sleep, the more jelly added to the nerves associated with that skill. The more jelly insulating your skill-related nerves, the more efficient and powerful and precise your completion of the task becomes.

Practice, then sleep, so your brain can work its nerve-jelly magic.

Cheetah Speed

Anthony Holler, mentioned at the end of *Chapter 2*, says "sprinters are cats." He wrote an excellent article about this topic for Freelap USA.[16]

Coach Holler's point is that sprinters run fast, win, then go to sleep. From house cats to cheetahs, cats run fast, eat their prey, then go to sleep. If you want to be one of the fast athletes, you have to run fast, win, then go to sleep. Winning is catching discs, getting blocks, or improving your time.

You cannot possibly become fast by running slow, so stop your practice session when your speed falls off. This happens _long before_ your legs or lungs feel tired. Speed is not endurance. Speed is not

---

[16] Links may change; search for "Tony Holler feed the cats speed training" if you want to read the article. Follow him on Twitter @pntrack.

strength. Speed is electricity. When that electric circuit overheats, coordination declines, you slow down, and your brain doesn't receive a signal to add myelin, the insulating jelly, to your running circuit.

Ultimately, speed training gets boiled down to "run fast to become fast," with a nod to decent technique. You may struggle to practice running technique with focus and intensity once it becomes boring. You may struggle to chase discs, opponents, or seconds when the novelty of competition wears off. You may long for the ache, burn, and satisfaction of endurance training when your early gains dry up.

It is simple to become fast, but difficult to stay the course.

Trees continue *trying* to grow year after year. Some years, there is drought and others there is rain; some years the soil is baked by the sun and others the soil is well-nourished. There will be thin rings and thick rings which mark the tree's growth.

The same can be said of your speed's growth. In the beginning, you will tend to your seeds (technique) and will keep up your soil (competition) and will provide nourishment (sleep) to your speed tree. But there will be sloppy reps, there will be lazy efforts, and there will be late nights. This, more than any other reason, is why speed grows so slowly.

But if you have come this far, you are committed. Just as you have spent years perfecting your inside-out backhand, you can spend years improving your speed. You are either too determined or too stubborn to be discouraged. For you, it's time to make a plan. A plan to become fast. That's up next.

Chapter 4:
Becoming A Fast Kid

Speed Never Expires

The magic of this book is not its training programs. Training programs are available all over the Internet. *6 Weeks To This* and *30 Days To That*. Those training programs are exhausting, difficult, and loaded with novel exercises. After every session, you tend to be a sweaty mess, sore for multiple days, and satisfied emotionally with the variety they provide. However, as Dan John likes to say of a popular 90-day exercise series, "What do you do on Day 91?"

Most training programs have an expiration date. Speed development does not have an expiration date. Developing speed is like growing a tree! Bamboo trees can grow up to one inch per hour, yet they still require at least five years to reach maturity.

The principles of training for speed presented in this book will last you several years. You may be bored, but it will deliver. You may not be sore, but it will deliver. You may feel underworked, but it will deliver. As I said earlier in the book, I wish I had the audacity to make speed seem complicated.

In order to become faster and apply that speed on the field, there are three stages to your year of training: monthly performance testing in the offseason, training your weaknesses between performance tests, and maintaining your skills during the season. Players at ATX Speed have used these exact principles and these exact exercises since 2015 in order to get more blocks and shake more defenders.

Honest assessment

You know where you want to go. You have already committed to the long road ahead. But we cannot jump into a training program without knowing where, exactly, you are beginning. We need numbers which predict how much faster you could be, insight about the qualities holding you back, and data points to track over time. Every month, we will test these numbers to see if your weaknesses are improving. When these tests improve, speed improves.

Posture Tests

Achieving the Hard Z position while running fast requires the strength to hold great posture while absorbing and producing large forces. This first set of tests will reveal if you have the strength to hold great posture *without* external forces to be absorbed.

Hip Lock

Vern Gambetta, former strength & conditioning coach for the White Sox, suggested "teaching to the test" when coaching speed technique. Since the test of your Hard Z is the hip lock, in order to improve it, you will practice the hip lock.

In this position, with your hands on your hips, your support foot is flat on the ground, your support knee is straight, your swing leg knee is above your hip, and you lift your swing-side hip bone as high in the air as you can, then hold (version 1). Time how long you can maintain this position, then test the other side.

Hip Lock, version 1

As you gain strength and stability, place your hands behind your head (version 2).

Hip Lock, version 2

Eventually, hold a broomstick overhead (version 3).

Hip Lock, version 3

Hollow-body Position

The hip lock assessed your ability to tilt your bowl (your hips) from left-to-right using your butt muscles. The hollow-body position, by contrast, assesses your ability to tilt your bowl front-to-back using your stomach and low back muscles. This strength is helpful for relieving back pain which results from sitting, so many players will benefit from that alone. This strength is also critical for optimal stride length at top speed.

In this position, your priority is to keep your lower back pressed firmly flat against the ground. In the beginning, tuck your knees to your chest and hold your arms at your sides (version 1).

Hollow-body Position, version I

As you gain strength, lengthen the lever by reaching your feet and hands up into the air (version 2).

Hollow-body Position, version 2

Eventually, measure the full hollow-body position by reaching your feet and toes far apart (version 3).

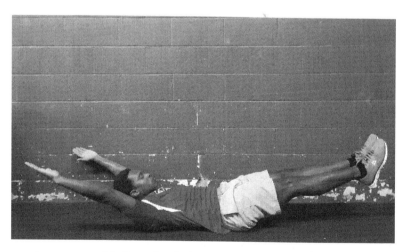

Hollow-body Position, version 3

Static Split Squat

Running fast requires the flexibility to split your thighs far apart, with one thigh parallel to the ground and the other thigh angled behind your hips. The static split squat assesses your ability to create thigh separation by both measuring and training this flexibility.

In this position, set up in a long lunge, keeping your toes pointed straight forward. Sink down into the split squat (version 1). Stop when your knee is just off the floor. If your front knee is forward of your ankle bone, lengthen your split squat stance. Time how long you can hold this position, then test the other side.

Static Split Squat, version 1, start & finish

As flexibility improves, put your foot onto a 12" (30cm) box (version 2).

Static Split Squat, version 2, start & finish

Eventually, place your back foot flat onto a knee-high box (version 3).

Power Tests

The posture tests measure your ability to execute the Hard Z position. The other key component to running technique was stiff ankles. Remember, stiff ankles actually refers to efficient and explosive lower leg muscles. These power tests measure your lower legs' explosiveness and efficiency.

Static Split Squat, version 3, start & finish

Standing Broad Jump

When defending a handler loosely, perhaps in a zone defense or while disrupting a dump set, you will likely have to jump off two feet in order to knock down a disc. Since that jump is rarely straight up, the vertical jump is a poor indicator of your ability to make that play. The broad jump also quantifies your jumping ability and is more specific to ultimate.

With your feet hip-width apart, drop your hips while swinging your arms back, then jump as far forward as you can. This test is measured from where your toes began to where your heels land. If your feet land staggered, use the back-most heel for measurement. Make three attempts. Record your longest jump and the average of your two best jumps.

Standing Broad Jump

Standing Three Jump

Acceleration up to top speed depends on many reflexes. The key function of those reflexes is to make your torso very stiff in order to rebound forces your body absorbs into the ground. The three jump is the lowest-impact test for assessing how efficiently you convert your broad jump -- *strength needed to accelerate* -- to elastic power -- *stiffness needed to run fast.*

This test is simply three consecutive broad jumps, without pausing to reset in between landings. There is a rhythm to the three jump. Make a full-foot landing, sink into your optimal jumping position, and take off into the next jump within about half a second (0.5 seconds). This test is measured from where your toes began before the first jump to where your heels land after the third jump. Again, if one heel lands farther back than the other, use the farthest back heel for measurement. Make three attempts. Record your longest jump and the average of your two best jumps.

Lateral 1-leg Hops

You must master the Hard Z position and build reactive legs in order to run well at top speed. Remember the video of David Oliver's heel freezing in space during acceleration? That's a reactive leg. Lateral hops assess and train the ability of your muscles to react effectively to the ground.

Stand on one leg with a dome cone to the inside of your foot. Hop back and forth over the cone as fast as you can. If you hit the cone and it moves, restart the test. Count every landing in 10 seconds. After hopping and recording your total count, test the other side.

Speed Tests

In training, you created a competitive environment so that your running is at true 100% intensity. If you ran down discs, you relied upon the thrower to give you slightly harder targets each rep. If you chased another player, you relied upon your training partner to go all-out and you progressively gave them larger head starts each practice session. While both of these environments will produce speed gains, they do not measure them.

The only way to prove that your speed is improving is to time sprints. I have timed over 1,000 sprints by ultimate players, doz-

1-leg Lateral Hop

ens per individual player spread over two years. That data is how I know the program presented in this book will make you faster. The program has already worked for over 100 players: league, college, club, & semi-pro.

The challenge of timing your sprints is the role of human error on accuracy. 10-meter flying sprints are ideal for measuring top speed. But they require electronic timing equipment in order to get accurate times, since great flying 10s are 1.10 seconds or shorter. Every hundredth of a second (0.01 seconds) is significant in the flying 10. If you love training technology, invest in the system ATX Speed athletes use every week.[17]

If $1,400 electronics are outside of your budget, however, we can simply extend your test distance. Longer test distances do not measure true top speed, but they do produce reliable benchmarks for

---

[17] Freelap Athletic Timing Systems: http://simplifaster.com/store/

your speed. They also provide more increments of time by which to measure improvement.

Self-timing with a stopwatch is good enough, so long as the distance run is long enough to minimize the impact of human error. After lots of practice, human error is estimated as +/- 0.2 seconds. Any speed test lasting longer than three seconds will have an acceptable amount of human error. As long as the same person operates the timer on every rep (you!), the error will be consistent and will not affect long-term testing.[18]

Our speed tests are simple. You can choose either a 40 yard dash from a standing start or a 30 yard flying sprint.

Standing 40

Use a standard mark like a yard line on a football field as a start line. Place two pyramid cones side-by-side, one yard apart, 39 yards and 2 feet (119 feet)* from the start line. Place two more pyramid cones side-by-side, one yard apart, 40 yards and 1 feet (121 feet)* from the start line.

Stand with your right toes immediately behind the starting line and your left toes 4-6 inches[19] behind your right heel. Hinge at the waist and lean your entire body forward until it feels like you will fall.

Push hard off your right foot and start your stopwatch when your left foot hits the ground. Stop your stopwatch when any part of your body is within the box formed by your four large cones.

> *for users of metric units, you will test a standing 30 meter sprint. Your first pair of cones should be at 29.5 meters and your second pair of cones at 30.5 meters. See the tables in the Testing Standards section for more information.

---

[18] *Accuracy* matters less than *consistency*. If your error is consistent, changes in time from week to week demonstrate progress.

[19] 10-15 centimeters

Time three runs, resting 4 minutes rest between runs. Record your best overall time and the average of the three times.

Flying 30

Place two pyramid cones side-by-side, one yard apart, 30 yards (90 feet)* from any appropriate starting line. Place two more pyramid cones side-by-side, one yard apart, 60 yards (180 feet)* from the starting line.

Stand with your right toes immediately behind the starting line and your left toes 4-6 inches[20] behind your right heel. Hinge at the waist and lean your entire body forward until it feels like you will fall.

Push hard off your right foot and gradually rise up to your full height before the first set of cones. Start your stopwatch when any part of your body passes between the first set of cones. Stop your stopwatch when any part of your body passes between the second set of cones.

> *if you measure distance in meters, you will test a flying 30 meter sprint. Your first pair of cones should be at 30 meters and your second pair of cones at 60 meters. See the tables in the Testing Standards section for more information.*

Time three runs, resting 6 minutes rest between runs. Record your best overall time and the average of the three times.

How to Test

In the final week of each training program, there are prescribed rest days and easy training days. On test day, complete the Mobility Warmup (presented in *Appendix A*), then your posture tests in this order:

● Hip Lock hold
   30 seconds of rest after each side

---

[20] 10-15 centimeters

- Hollow-body Position hold
  1 minute of rest
- Static Split Squat hold
  30 seconds of rest between sides

If you meet the top performance standard for Version 1 or Version 2 *on both sides* for a posture test, take the prescribed rest, then test Version 2 or Version 3 as appropriate before moving to the next posture test.

Next, go to the field and set up the cones for your timed sprint. Complete the Speed Warmup, then your power tests in this order:

- Standing Broad Jump
  30 seconds of rest after each attempt
- Standing Three Jump
  1 minute of rest after each attempt
- 1-leg Lateral Hops
  30 seconds of rest between sides

Finally, report to the appropriate start position of your timed sprint and test as described.

Testing Standards

The speed tests will reveal your progress toward becoming a fast kid. Expect to see your *average* performance improve at every monthly test. Your best overall sprint times may not improve at every test, but should improve by the end of offseason and in each subsequent offseason.

After two years of performance testing on ultimate players and five years of performance testing on athletes from other sports, I have the data to present Poor, Average, Good, and Great performances for each of these tests. The tables below are grouped by gender, arranged vertically by the tests in the order presented above, and arranged horizontally from poor performance to great performance in each test.

Women's Standards Table

Test	Poor	Average	Good	Great
Hip lock	Version 1 (V1) <30 seconds (sec)	V1 60 sec	V2 60 sec OR V3 30 sec	V3 60 sec
Hollow-body	V1 <30 sec	V1 60 sec	V2 60 sec OR V3 30 sec	V3 60 sec
Split squat	V1 <30 sec	V1 30 sec	V2 30 sec	V3 30 sec
Broad jump	< 1.10	≤ 1.25	≤ 1.50	> 1.50
Three jump	≤ 3.00	≤ 3.50	≤ 4.25	> 4.25
1-leg hops	< 20	< 24	< 28	≥ 28
Standing 40yd	> 5.55 sec	≤ 5.55 sec	≤ 5.35 sec	≤ 5.15 sec
Flying 30yd	> 3.90 sec	≤ 3.90 sec	≤ 3.60 sec	≤ 3.30 sec
Standing 30m	> 4.65 sec	≤ 4.65 sec	≤ 4.45 sec	≤ 4.25 sec
Flying 30m	> 4.00 sec	≤ 4.00 sec	≤ 3.75 sec	≤ 3.50 sec

Men's Standards Table

Test	Poor	Average	Good	Great
Hip lock	Version 1 (V1) <30 seconds (sec)	V1 60 sec	V2 60 sec OR V3 30 sec	V3 60 sec
Hollow-body	V1 <30 sec	V1 60 sec	V2 60 sec OR V3 30 sec	V3 60 sec
Split squat	V1 <30 sec	V1 30 sec	V2 30 sec	V3 30 sec
Broad jump	≤ 1.20	≤ 1.35	≤ 1.50	> 1.50
Three jump	≤ 3.50	≤ 4.00	≤ 4.50	> 4.50
1-leg hops	< 20	< 24	< 28	≥ 28
Standing 40yd	> 5.20 sec	≤ 5.20 sec	≤ 5.05 sec	≤ 4.90 sec
Flying 30yd	> 3.50 sec	≤ 3.50 sec	≤ 3.35 sec	≤ 3.15 sec
Standing 30m	> 4.50 sec	≤ 4.50 sec	≤ 4.30 sec	≤ 4.10 sec
Flying 30m	> 3.65 sec	≤ 3.65 sec	≤ 3.50 sec	≤ 3.35 sec

Discussion of Standards

The posture tests, speed tests, and lateral hop test are probably easy to understand. The jumps, however, require some explanation. The broad jump standard is normalized, which means its value accounts for some other factor. Height has the largest impact on broad jump ability, before power can be measured. In this book, the broad jump standard reflects distance jumped divided by athlete height. For example, if a 5 foot 6 inch player jumps 7 feet 0 inches, their normalized standing broad jump is 84 inches divided by 66 inches or 1.27.[21] [22]

The three jump is also normalized. Traditionally, the three jump is described relative to broad jump distance (distance jumped divided by distance jumped). However, to make progress more obvious, in this book, the three jump also reflects distance jumped divided by athlete height. For example, if the same 5 foot 6 inch player jumps 20 feet 6 inches, their normalized three jump is 246 inches divided by 66 inches or 3.73.

Both broad jump distance and three jump distance will increase with training. You would notice your own progress just from these jump numbers. But in order to compare jumps across different players, height must be accounted for. Also, because your broad jump influences your three jump, the ratio of the two could stay the same.

Over time, because we use athlete height as the standard candle against which to measure jumping performance, these normalized numbers will both improve at each monthly test for at least one off-season and you can compare your jump to your teammate's jump, regardless of her height.

---

[21] Ratios are quantities with no units, so it does not matter if you measure your jumps in Imperial or in metric distances. For example, if a 168 cm player jumps 2.13 m, their normalized standing broad jump is still 1.27.

[22] 1.27 means you jumped 27% farther than you are tall. It lets us quantify explosiveness while accounting for body size. It is not an exact measurement, but it is useful and simple to calculate.

Using Test Results to Select a Training Program

In the offseason, your task is to improve your weaknesses so that speed can also improve. To determine which offseason training program to use, let's do a quick analysis of your performance tests.

The first six tests were presented in the order of their importance. The training programs are grouped by the qualities each test represents. Your speed test selection does not influence which training program you need.

Choose the Design Posture program if you had:

- A Poor performance in any of the three posture tests
- A Poor performance in the standing broad jump test
- Your lowest overall performance in any of these tests

Choose the Quick Feet program if you do not require the Design Posture program and had:

- A Poor performance in the three jump or lateral hop tests
- Your lowest overall performance in one or both of these tests

Choose the All-Around program if your performances in all six tests were at the same level.

Training Programs for (Future) Fast Kids

For now, there is nothing more to learn. Based on your test results, pick a program, then get to work. Each month, new test results will determine which program you use in the subsequent month.

The warmup sequences are provided in Appendix A: Warmup Routines.

The exercises used in these training programs are demonstrated in videos on the unlisted YouTube playlist Fast Kids Dont Train Slow Exercises.[23]

---

[23] *Fast Kids Dont Train Slow exercises* at http://atxspeedandstrength.com/resources/FKDTS

Training Program: Design Posture

DESIGN POSTURE	Week 1	Week 2
Monday		
Tuesday	Speed warmup A1: Leg scissor hop V1 5 x 20yd A2: Bounding 5 x 20yd B: competitive sprints x until performance declines	Speed warmup A1: Leg scissor hop V1 4 x 30yd A2: Bounding 4 x 30yd B: competitive sprints x until performance declines
Wednesday	Mobility warmup A1: kneeling switch V1 4 x 10 A2: Leg scissor V1 4 x (20 x 1)	Mobility warmup A1: kneeling switch V2 3 x 10 A2: Leg scissor V1 double 3 x (6 x 2) R/L
Thursday	Strength warmup A: 1-leg deadlift 3 x 8 R/L B1: split squat 5 x 8 R/L B2: hanging leg lift (HLL) 5 x 5	Strength warmup A: 1-leg deadlift 3 x 8 R/L B1: split squat 5 x 10 R/L B2: HLL 5 x 8
Friday		
Saturday	Speed warmup A: competitive sprints x until performance declines	Speed warmup A: competitive sprints x until performance declines
Sunday	Strength warmup A: 1-leg deadlift 5 x 5 R/L B1: step-up 8 x 4 R/L B2: box jump 8 x 4	Strength warmup A: 1-leg deadlift 5 x 5 R/L B1: step-up 6 x 5 R/L B2: box jump 6 x 4

DESIGN POSTURE	Week 3	Week 4
Monday		
Tuesday	Speed warmup A1: Leg scissor hop V1 double 3 x 20yd R/L A2: Bounding 3 x 30yd B: competitive sprints x until performance declines	Speed warmup A1: Leg scissor hop V1 triple 3 x 30yd A2: Bounding 3 x 30yd A3: Strides 3 x test distance
Wednesday	Mobility warmup A1: kneeling switch V2 3 x 10 A2: leg scissor V1 triple 3 x (8 x 3)	Mobility warmup Strength warmup A1: kneeling switch V2 3 x 10 A2: split squat 3 x 10 R/L A3: HLL 3 x 10
Thursday	Strength warmup A: 1-leg deadlift 3 x 8 R/L B1: split squat 5 x 10 R/L B2: HLL 5 x 10	OFF
Friday		Test warmup
Saturday	Speed warmup A: competitive sprints x until performance declines	Test warmup TEST
Sunday	Strength warmup A: 1-leg deadlift 5 x 5 R/L B1: step-up 5 x 8 R/L B2: box jump 5 x 5	OFF

Training Program: Quick Feet

QUICK FEET	Week 1	Week 2

Monday	Speed warmup
	A1: Uphill bounding
	    5 x 10 steps
	A2: Jump rope run
	    5 x 30yd
	B: Scramble start run
	    6 x 10yd
	C: Scramble start run
	    3 x 20yd
		Speed warmup
		A1: Uphill skip
		    5 x 20 steps
		A2: Jump rope run
		    5 x 30yd
		B: Scramble start run
		    4 x 10yd
		C: Scramble start run
		    4 x 20yd

Tuesday		

Wednesday	Speed warmup
	A1: 1-leg broad jump
	    4 x 3 R/L
	A2: quick feet on cone
	    4 x 30sec
	B: leg scissor V1 double
	    5 x (5 x 2) R/L
		Speed warmup
		A1: 1-leg broad jump
		    3 x 5 R/L
		A2: quick feet on cone
		    3 x 30sec
		B: leg scissor V2 double
		    5 x (5 x 2) R/L

Thursday		

Friday	Strength warmup
	A1: 1-leg deadlift 4 x 6
	    R/L
	A2: step-up switch 4 x 10
	A3: hanging leg lift (HLL)
	    4 x 6
		Strength warmup
		A1: 1-leg deadlift
		    4 x 6 R/L
		A2: step-up switch 4 x
		    10
		A3: HLL 4 x 8

Saturday	Speed warmup
	A1: A-skip 3 x 50yd
	A2: broad jump
	    3 x 5 jumps
	B: competitive sprints
	    x until performance
	    declines
		Speed warmup
		A1: A-skip 3 x 50yd
		A2: broad jump 3 x 5
		    jumps
		B: competitive sprints
		    x until performance
		    declines

Sunday		

QUICK FEET	Week 3	Week 4

Monday	Speed warmup
	A1: Uphill bounding
	   5 x 10 steps
	A2: Jump rope run
	   5 x 30yd
	B: Scramble start run
	   3 x 20yd
	C: Falling start run
	   3 x 30yd
		Speed warmup
		A1: Uphill skip
		   5 x 20 steps
		A2: Jump rope run
		   5 x 30yd
		B: Scramble start run
		   5 x 20yd
		C: Falling start run
		   4 x 30yd

Tuesday		

Wednesday	Speed warmup
	A1: 1-leg broad jump
	   5 x 5 R/L
	A2: quick feet on cone
	   5 x 30sec
	B: leg scissor V2 triple
	   5 x (8 x 3)
		Speed warmup
		A: Strides 5 x test distance

Thursday		OFF
Friday	Strength warmup A1: 1-leg deadlift 4 x 6 R/L A2: step-up switch 4 x 10 A3: HLL 4 x 10	Test warmup

Saturday	Speed warmup
	A1: A-skip 3 x 50yd
	A2: broad jump 3 x 5
	   jumps
	B: competitive sprints
	   x until performance
	   declines
		Test warmup
		TEST

Sunday		OFF

Training Program: All-Around

ALL-AROUND	Week 1	Week 2
Monday	Strength warmup A1: Medicine ball (MB) throw 10 x 5 or kettlebell (KB) swing 10 x 10 A2: box jump 10 x 3 B: split squat 5 x 8 R/L	Strength warmup A1: MB throw 10 x 5 or KB swing 10 x 10 A2: box jump 10 x 4 B: split squat 5 x 8 R/L
Tuesday	Speed warmup A1: jump rope run 5 x 30yd A2: scramble start run 5 x 20yd A3: hill sprint 5 x 10 steps	Speed warmup A1: competitive sprints x 5 A2: falling start run 5 x 20yd A3: hill bounding 5 x 6 steps
Wednesday	Mobility warmup Strength warmup A1: leg scissor V3 5 x (20 x 1) A2: Split squat switch 5 x 10 A3: Step-up 5 x 6 R/L	Mobility warmup Strength warmup A1: leg scissor V3 double 5 x (5 x 2) R/L A2: Split squat switch 5 x 10 A3: Step-up 5 x 6 R/L
Thursday		
Friday	Strength warmup A1: MB throw 5 x 10 or KB swing 5 x 15 A2: Rotation hop & box jump 5 x 3 R/L B: split squat 5 x 8 R/L	Strength warmup A1: MB throw 5 x 10 or KB swing 5 x 15 A2: Rotation hop & box jump 5 x 4 R/L B: split squat 5 x 8 R/L
Saturday	Speed warmup Competitive sprints x until performance declines	Speed warmup Competitive sprints x until performance declines
Sunday		

ALL-AROUND	Week 3	Week 4
Monday	Strength warmup A1: MB throw 10 x 5 or KB swing 10 x 10 A2: box jump 10 x 5 B: split squat 5 x 8 R/L	Strength warmup A1: MB throw 10 x 5 or KB swing 10 x 10 A2: box jump 10 x 5 B: split squat 5 x 8 R/L
Tuesday	Speed warmup A1: jump rope run 5 x 40yd A2: scramble start run 5 x 15yd A3: hill sprint 5 x 10 steps	Speed warmup A1: Strides 5 x test distance A2: falling start run 5 x 25yd A3: hill bounding 5 x 8 steps
Wednesday	Mobility warmup Strength warmup A1: leg scissor V3 triple 5 x (12 x 3) A2: Split squat switch 5 x 10 A3: Step-up 5 x 6 R/L	Mobility warmup Strength warmup A1: leg scissor V3 triple 3 x (14 x 3) A2: Split squat switch 3 x 8 A3: Step-up 3 x 6 R/L
Thursday		OFF
Friday	Strength warmup A1: MB throw 5 x 10 or KB swing 5 x 15 A2: Rotation hop & box jump 5 x 5 R/L B: Split squat 5 x 8 R/L	Test warmup
Saturday	Speed warmup Competitive sprints x until performance declines	Test warmup TEST
Sunday		OFF

Chapter 5:
Staying Fast During The Season

A Training Dilemma

The season stands before you like Mt. Everest. You have put in the time and the work. You know you are faster and more agile than you were last season. The mountain ahead represents many unanswered questions: How good will I really be? Will my teammates notice? What can I contribute to my team now? And the hardest question of them all...

With practices every week and tournaments every month, how will I keep training and making this sort of progress?

Randy Moss of the National Football League was renowned for his offseason training. He liked to show up to preseason training camp in the kind of shape that terrified rookies and shamed veterans. Everyone knew Moss would be stronger than the year before and faster than the year before and would make sharper cuts than the year before. They could hardly wait to see it for themselves.

Your situation is similar. You know you are better physically in many ways and you want your teammates to notice and, perhaps, envy your progress. You also want to keep growing, progressing, and building up those physical qualities. Progress is addicting! But if you pour more and more energy into your sprinting, there will not be much left for practicing game flow, implementing a playbook, or perfecting your throws under pressure.

You have a finite pool of energy. That energy has to be directed toward the main goal--playing ultimate. The thousands of meters run and hours of posture practice you have invested into being a better athlete were appetizers. The season is your main course. It is time to focus on conditioning, strategy, and playing. It is reasonable to want to preserve the gains you've made, but that is an impossible goal.

Preseason Conditioning for Ultimate

There was a warning at the beginning of this book:

*"This book **cannot** make you an all-star if you blindly pursue speed and neglect the myriad other skills it takes to play this game."*

Speed is a critical physical quality for elevating your ultimate game. You cannot be a true standout on any team that faces strong competition without it. But you need other qualities to succeed on the field. I am a sprinter and former weightlifter. I learned quickly that even a fast, powerful athlete cannot simply jump into ultimate, even a low-level game, and expect to have an impact.

Track workouts waste your energy. But you still need conditioning. Long runs are inappropriate for this sport. But you still need endurance. Most jumping workouts are ineffective. But you still need power. Bodybuilding methods reduce your speed. But you still need strength.

This section addresses those other qualities. First, we define how each quality applies to ultimate. Next, we try to quantify exactly how much of each quality is needed as an ultimate player. Finally, we explore a supplementary strength & conditioning program for the first month after tryouts to complete your preparation for the season.

About conditioning & endurance

This book dismissed track workouts and long runs as ineffective. You may have the impression that this book does not appreciate the roles endurance and conditioning play in ultimate. I made mistakes in my early days coaching ultimate players. I confessed to them in "The View From Out Here" in 2016, an article for online magazine Skyd. Since those early days, however, I have studied Nationals- and Worlds-level ultimate, watched dozens of hours of game film, and analyzed thousands of points. You do need conditioning to play this game. However, you probably need far less than you have been led to believe.

1. Not all conditioning is equal. "Work capacity" can refer to two qualities:
2. How much total work can be done without significant break

How often and how quickly total recovery can be accomplished between bouts of work

Highly-motivated players often confuse the two. They mistakenly believe conditioning that accomplishes the first also accomplishes the second. When I first met Johnny (not his real name), he was an endurance machine. He was a Work Capacity #1 zealot. Johnny ran between three and five miles every other morning. He arrived early to his team's weekly track workouts to practice 100-yard footwork drills. He jogged between 150-meter repeats. Johnny was most satisfied with practices when there were no subs during scrimmages.

But Johnny came to me for help: "I just can't keep up with my match-ups at the end of long points or on the second day. How can I get my endurance up?"

Johnny did not have an endurance problem. Johnny had a specificity problem. Perhaps you can relate. You may have the same problem.

The Requirements of Club Ultimate

In the mixed division of Club Nationals 2016, a typical[24] point lasted 45 seconds. Whether male or female, a typical handler made seven hard acceleration efforts during that time. Each acceleration was about six yards and lasted less than two seconds. That handler

---

[24] "Typical" is a catch-all term, reflecting that these are all mean values from the data I collected across 9 mixed games.

either walked or stood still between efforts. That handler typically played 11 points in each game.

In summary, a typical handler in the mixed division only ran hard during 14 of each point's 45 seconds. That handler needed about 77 accelerations over six yards during a game.

The Requirements of Semi-Pro Ultimate

Across two double-header weekends for the AUDL's Austin Sol in 2016, a typical offensive point lasted 20 seconds. A typical cutter made three efforts longer than 20 yards during that time. Each run lasted about two-and-a-half seconds. Between those efforts, that cutter mostly jogged or walked, except for several cut steps and power steps meant to pull a defender off-balance. That cutter typically played 23 points per game.

In summary, a typical cutter for Sol only ran hard during 8 of each point's 20 seconds. That cutter needed about 69 hard sprints in a game.

Think about Johnny: except while scrimmaging savage, when did his training prepare his body for 69 to 77 hard accelerations, alternated with standing, walking, or jogging rest? Johnny did not have an endurance problem. Johnny had a specificity problem. His training did not look like the demands of ultimate.

You need conditioning to play this game. However, you will not find the right type of conditioning in long jogs, 150-meter repeats, or the gym.

How Austin ultimate players condition

Long shuttle runs and on-the-minute (OTM) short sprints are the best practice sessions I have found for developing ultimate-specific endurance. Here are two sessions Austin Sol and Texas Showdown used in 2017.

1. Shuttle run: Out 20 yards and back, out 30 yards and back, out 40 yards and back, plus one 60 yard sprint out. Five runs with three minutes of rest between runs.

There are seven hard efforts per run.
There are 35 hard efforts per practice session.
Each run lasts between 40 and 50 seconds for fast players.
The conditioning session is complete in 17 minutes.

2. OTM sprints: Out 40 yards and back, five times. Start each sprint at the top of every minute. Three sets with two minutes of rest between sets.

There are 10 hard efforts per run.
There are 30 hard efforts per practice session.
Each run lasts between 12 and 15 seconds for fast players.
The conditioning session is complete in 19 minutes.

Each week, complete each session once and attend two team practices. In less than two months of training, you will learn to accelerate repeatedly with short recovery periods. You will adapt to the demands of ultimate. No 10 x 200-meter sessions; no 45-minute hill workouts; no suffering for its own sake. Just training that looks and feels like the game.

About power, jumping, and plyos

In early 2017, an Austin physical therapist and I discussed injuries in ultimate. It was her ninth season as a women's club player. She noted that in each of those nine seasons, at least one of her teammates suffered a catastrophic knee injury. She also noted that on every team she played for, at least three players suffered from shin splints. She wondered aloud if players tend to run and jump too much with inadequate preparation and improper technique. I wondered if doing so was just part of the culture.

Perhaps you have experienced a wrenched knee or, worse, an ACL or MCL surgery. Perhaps you have struggled with shin splints in the early season, plantar fasciitis at mid-season, or sharp Achilles pain late in the season. Leslie (not her real name) felt all of the above when I met her. She could walk fine most of the time, but the day after track workouts, her heels and shins were painful to the touch. Her ankles were very stiff the morning after practices. Leslie was three weeks out from her first tournament of the year and concerned she would not be healthy enough to play.

We could not resolve her pain on such a short deadline. We could find its source and minimize tissue damage so she would be healthy enough to compete. I reviewed her training program. She had an individual track workout on Monday. That workout was a pyramid session: 400m, 300m, 200m, 100m, 200m, 300m, 400m, with "just a few seconds of rest" between runs. She had team practices on Tuesday and Saturday. She lifted upper body weights at her gym Wednesday and Friday.

I asked Leslie about her warmups, cool downs, and self-care after training. She described a long "plyo warmup" that she used every training day -- Monday at the track workout, Tuesday at practice, Wednesday at the gym, Friday at the gym, and Saturday at practice. She did not cool down after most practices. Self-care was foam rolling her calves and shins after weekend practice. Perhaps you have used a similar weekly schedule.

Too Much of a Good Thing

Plyometrics might be the most abused training methods in sports. No athletes and very few coaches know what it means anymore. The original Russian term meant drops off tall boxes, either to stuck landings or to quick rebound jumps. The plyometric training method was meant to teach the body to rebound harder using the stretch-shortening cycle of connective tissues. Today, the term plyometrics seems to refer to all skipping, hopping, running, jumping, and explosive movements.

If we accept plyometric training to mean all stretch-shorten movements, we can apply research-based recommendations about how much plyometric work is safe. A typical recommendation comes from sport scientist by Nikolay Ozolin regarding depth jumps: "up to 15 reps per session from moderate heights, with at most two sessions per week if you are not in a strength cycle."

A different recommendation comes from exercise physiologist Dr. Mel Siff regarding all hops and jumps: "take care not to exceed 50 foot contacts of intense means in a week of training; perhaps 150 or 200 contacts of remedial means."

And track coach Charlie Francis made the argument in the mid-80s that "jump training is of secondary importance to the sprinter; one session each week of 20-30 easy jumps will suffice."

Look at Leslie's training. The tally of stretch-shortening cycle-dependant activities is enormous. There were jumps in the warmup five days per week, seven long sprints at track, and two days of practice. Based on Dr. Siff's definitions in Supertraining, there were 30 remedial foot contacts in her warmup alone. She performed the full prescription of 150 jumps per week before running a single step! It should be obvious why her legs hurt the day after track workouts and practices.

Playing is Training, Too

In ultimate, as described in the conditioning section, most players will accelerate 70 times in a game. Based on two years of observing Texas Showdown and Austin Sol, players will make a similar number of efforts in a two-hour practice. Every sprinting step is a plyometric action.

Most players will also jump several times during play, whether two-foot jumps for party balls, one-foot takeoffs to bid for a disc, or hops to catch a disc slightly out of reach. I do not have enough data to present average numbers. Your experience in the sport probably supports that players will jump at least once on every point. Every jump is a plyometric action.[25]

Every single point you will ever play in this game is full of plyometric actions. To avoid overuse injuries, most players should not perform any additional jump training during the season. The preseason transition program offered in this section includes no jumping except for the skips and simple hops in your warmups.

You want to be available to play when it is time to compete. You will enjoy your season more if you are healthy and enthusiastic instead of achy, tired, and worried about devastating injury.

Curious about Leslie? We cut out her track sessions and removed all the jumping from her warmup. She took hot and cold baths daily, worked on her ankle flexibility, and used stationary bikes and rowing machines for interval-based conditioning. She did not run another track session that season. When it was time to play, somehow she was still a strong defensive handler who knocked down at least one disc per game. After a disappointing loss in quarters at Nationals that year, she noticed something: for the first time in over a year, her shins didn't hurt.

---

[25] Technical correction: every landing is a plyometric action; every jump is merely an explosive one.

Training Program: Preseason Transition

TRANSITION	Week 1	Week 2
Monday		
Tuesday	Speed warmup A1: scramble start 　run 5 x 10yd A2: falling start 　run 5 x 30yd B: flying run 3 x 30yd C: OTM sprints 2 x 5 　x 50yd	Speed warmup A1: falling start 　run 4 x 20yd A2: standing start 　run 4 x 40yd B: flying run 2 x 　30yd C: OTM sprints 　3 x 5 x 40yd
Wednesday	Team Practice	Team Practice
Thursday		
Friday	Strength warmup A1: MB throw 5 x 5 　or KB swing 5 x 10 A2: ankle ABCs B1: split squat 　3 x 8 R/L B2: hollow-body hold 　3 x 45sec C: 1-leg deadlift 　4 x 6 R/L	Strength warmup A1: MB throw 5 x 5 　or KB swing 5 x 10 A2: ankle ABCs B1: split squat 　4 x 6 R/L B2: hollow-body 　hold 4 x 45sec C: 1-leg deadlift 　4 x 6 R/L
Saturday	Team Practice	Team Practice
Sunday		

TRANSITION	Week 3	Week 4
Monday		
Tuesday	Speed warmup A1: scramble start run 3 x 15yd A2: flying run 3 x 30yd B: OTM sprints 2 x 5 x 40yd C: shuttle run 2 x 10-20-30yd	Speed warmup A1: falling start run 3 x 20yd A2: flying run 3 x 30yd C: shuttle run 3 x 20-30-40yd
Wednesday	Team Practice	Team Practice
Thursday		
Friday	Strength warmup A1: ankle ABCs A2: split squat 5 x 5 R/L A3: hollow-body hold 5 x 45sec B1: 1-leg deadlift 4 x 6 R/L B2: step-up 4 x 10	Strength warmup A1: ankle ABCs A2: split squat 5 x 5 R/L B1: 1-leg deadlift 5 x 5 R/L B2: step-up 5 x 8 R/L C1: hollow-body hold 2 x 1min C2: hanging leg lift 2 x 15
Saturday	Team Practice	Team Practice
Sunday		

In-season Training

The season is a war of attrition. If you keep speed as your primary goal, then the season will grind you with mid-week practices, weekend camps, and two or three-day tournaments every four weeks. It will wear you down if you try to train three days each week on top of that practice load.

If, however, you set the season as your primary goal, you can focus on playing well and utilizing the speed you have built to do so. Instead of fretting over not continuing to progress, do the minimum necessary work to maintain what you have built. In-season training relates to offseason training the way watering a young tree every day relates to planting, aerating, and fertilizing it as a seed.

Do just enough to keep the tree alive!

It is necessary to train speed less during the season. As a rule of thumb, you can do half the training you did in the offseason, taking just one day to sprint, and most of the progress you made will stay in place. The in-season training plan in this section combined with the preseason transition program in the previous section will help.

Long-term Speed Development

If you focus on your athletic major (the season) and stay reasonable about your athletic minor (speed development) then you will have a great competitive year. Do not stop trying to be a well-rounded athlete in-season. Instead, use the gains you made in the offseason to be a better player when it counts. Do just enough supporting work to minimize your losses. Take comfort in two biological facts: (1) it is easier to recover qualities you have lost than it is to build them originally; (2) next year's progress will be built on top of this year's progress.

Take a long view of your training. Perhaps you have achieved 60% of your potential as a speed demon this year. The season will deplete your capacity somewhat, then you will spend two or three weeks catching up in the offseason. But you will probably start next season at 75% of your potential. And the year after that, perhaps 80 or 85%. And in every subsequent year of focused training using the principles revealed in this book, you will become better at focused training.

You will become faster year after year as a result.

Every day, every week, every month, and every year you invest into intelligent training for ultimate is like practice baking a cake. No need to hoard the one you have made this offseason —the next cake will look and taste even better. To me, that is something to get excited about. Now go enjoy yourself in the competitive season.

Training Program: In-Season Maintenance

MAINTENANCE	Normal Week	Camp / Tournament Week
Monday		
Tuesday	Mobility warmup Speed warmup A1: scramble start run 3 x 15yd A2: jump rope run 3 x 30yd B: flying sprint 3 x 30yd C: long shuttle or OTM sprints	Mobility warmup Speed warmup A1: A-skip 4 x 50yd A2: jump rope run 4 x 50yd B: hill sprint 8 x 10 steps
Wednesday	Team Practice	Team Practice
Thursday		(Optional day) Mobility warmup Strength warmup A1: split squat 5 x 5 R/L A2: hanging leg lift 5 x 10
Friday	Mobility warmup Strength warmup A1: step-up 5 x 8 R/L A2: hollow-body hold 5 x 30sec A3: forearm plank 5 x 1min	
Saturday	Team Practice	Camp / Competition
Sunday		Camp / Competition

Conclusion:
Don't Ever Train Slow

The Impact of Speed (reprise)

There is so much more to playing ultimate than running fast. You have to read the field, control your match-up, flow with your team, and know what to do with the disc under pressure. There is strategy to execute, specific conditioning to survive tournaments, footwork to get open, and collision on every layout. And yet, without the special something of speed, you may never have the opportunity to be competitive in all those other ways.

Most athletes and most coaches believe speed is innate. They think it cannot be taught, cannot be developed, and cannot be improved. You have it or you don't.

Most athletes and most coaches are wrong.

Speed is a skill, just like throwing an accurate scoober or forcing a high backhand on the mark. The trouble with speed is that it is not strength, it is not endurance, and it is not conditioning. Speed is electricity. Speed has to be felt to be understood. Slow coaches and slow athletes cannot see what makes speed possible and have not felt what makes speed possible, so they cannot understand what makes it possible.

But you have the tools now. You understand the posture which speed requires and the strength that supports it. You understand the coordination which speed requires and the neural system which facilitates it. You understand the commitment which speed requires and the training which maximizes it. You have the knowledge necessary to run faster. Now you have to invest the time.

Speed grows like a tree. Do not be dissatisfied with ¼- or ½-a-second improvement in your speed tests after the first offseason of training. The sapling would not be dissatisfied to have broken out of the dirt one year after its planting. One day the tree will stretch to the sky. One day you may be the player no one can catch. Appreciate progress already made.

Speed grows like a tree. Do not beat yourself up if you struggle with the process or fall out of habit every now and then. The tree would not beat itself up because there are occasional years of drought. Some rings will be thin and some will be thick. Some months you will improve by leaps and some months you will improve by baby steps. But every year has growth.

Speed grows like a tree. Do not worry if you are not yet the fastest on your team. The tree does not concern itself with the forest which surrounds it. Other trees will wither. Other players will retire. You will have your opportunity to be noticed.

Plant your seeds, cultivate your soil, and nurture your speed tree. When the season arrives, having invested your time into focused training, go put your speed to use on the field where it matters most. There will always be another offseason to become faster still.

That is the most liberating fact of all. You really can't teach tall...but if speed can be built, then today is the time to begin following this map to becoming one of the fast kids. Now you know the how, the what, the when, and the where of becoming faster.

The why? Because there are hucks to be run down, Ds to be had, and defenders to leave in your dust. Because you want to get open more often, more easily, and more consistently. Because you want to be the all-star on your team who everyone can rely on to chase errant throws and make game-saving catches.

Remember: The "who" of speed? That is YOU.

Get to work. And don't ever train slow.

Appendix A:
Warmup Routines

Training Program: Mobility Warmup

Exercise	Duration
Leg raise	10 repetitions (reps)
Hip bridge	10 reps
Lying leg swing	5 reps per side
Figure-4 hip bridge	5 reps per side
Scorpion twist	5 reps per side
Fire hydrant	5 reps per side
Heel lift	5 reps per side
Lateral swing	5 reps per side
Lizard stretch	15 seconds per side
Wide-legged pike-to-arch	10 reps

For links to exercise demonstrations, visit
http://atxspeedandstrength.com/resources/FKDTS

Training Program: Strength Warmup

Exercise	Duration
Back extension	10 reps
Bird-dog	5 reps per side
Cross-body mountain climber	5 reps per side
Pushup	10 reps
Bridging leg swing	5 reps per side
Lunge	5 reps per side
Squat	10 reps
Inchworm	5 reps

For links to exercise demonstrations, visit
http://atxspeedandstrength.com/resources/FKDTS

Training Program: Speed Warmup

Exercise	Duration
Heel walk	15 yards
Leg-across-body pull	15 yards
Walking toe touch	15 yards
Spiderman crawl	15 yards
Backward skip	15 yards
A-skip	15 yards
Straight-leg run	30 yards
High knees run	30 yards
Easy acceleration	30 yards
Hard acceleration	30 yards

For links to exercise demonstrations, visit
http://atxspeedandstrength.com/resources/FKDTS

Training Program: Test Warmup

Exercise	Duration
Mobility warmup	Before Posture Tests
Speed warmup	Before Power Tests
	Speed Test follows Power Tests

For links to exercise demonstrations, visit
http://atxspeedandstrength.com/resources/FKDTS

.

Appendix B:
Exercise Descriptions

The Fast Kids Dont Train Slow Exercises video playlist of training exercise demonstrations is available on YouTube for your reference.

Visit http://atxspeedandstrength.com/resources/FKDTS for links.

Test Exercises

- **Hard Z**
  1-leg stance with swing knee hip-high and arms in running positions

- **Hip Lock**
  Single-leg stance, as an assessment of posture

- **Hollow-body Position**
  Laying on back with pelvis tilted backward, an assessment of torso strength

- **Split Squat**
  Static lunge position, an assessment of hip flexibility

- **Standing Broad Jump**
  Jumping as far forward as you can from a standing start, an assessment of power

- **Standing Three Jump**
  Three consecutive broad jumps, an assessment of elastic power

- **1-leg Lateral Hops**
  Jumping left-and-right over a 2" cone, an assessment of lower leg reactive power

- **40yd/30m Standing Start Sprint**
  Timed running test from a standing start, an assessment of acceleration & top speed

- **30yd/30m Flying Start Sprint**
  Timed running test from a running start, an assessment of top speed & coordination

Appendix C:
Suggested Reading

This is not the first book written about speed development. It is the first to bring speed training into the context of ultimate. The books below will lead the inquiring reader deeper into the rabbit hole of human performance. Entries are listed with the author's name, the title underlined, and the year of publication. Most of these books are available on Amazon.

On Speed Development

- Frans Bosch & Ronald Klomp, Running (2004)
- Charlie Francis, The Charlie Francis Training System (1992)
- Travis Hansen, The Speed Encyclopedia (2015)
- Steve Magness, The Science of Running (2014)
- Charles Paddock, Track and Field (1933)
- Fred Wilt, How They Train volume 3 (1973)
- Bud Winter, So You Want To Be A Sprinter (1973)

On Strength & Conditioning

- Frans Bosch, Strength Training and Coordination (2012)
- Dan John & Pavel Tsatsouline, Easy Strength (2011)
- Dan John, Intervention (2012)
- Dr. Mel Siff, Supertraining 5th ed. (2000)
- Joel Smith, Vertical Foundations (2014)
- Joel Smith, Vertical Ignition (2015)

On Skill Development

- Daniel Coyle, The Talent Code (2009)
- David Epstein, The Sports Gene (2013)
- K. Anders Ericsson & Robert Pool, Peak (2016)
- Malcolm Gladwell, Outliers (2008)

On Fast Kids

- Usain Bolt, Faster Than Lightning (2013)
- Charlie Francis, Speed Trap (1991)
- Samuel Hawley, I Just Ran: Percy Williams (2011)
- Michael Johnson, Gold Rush (2011)
- Dan O'Brien, Clearing Hurdles (2012)
- Jackie Joyner-Kersee, A Kind of Grace (1999)

On Tactics & Strategy in Ultimate

- Michael Baccarini, Essential Ultimate (2008)
- James Parinella, Ultimate Technique and Tactics (2004)

About The Author

Dunte Hector is the owner and head coach at ATX Speed. He specializes in helping ultimate players run faster, jump higher, and play harder. He jokes that half of what he knows came from Dan John & Pavel Tsatsouline's Easy Strength and the other half is still under development. He is a self-taught strength & conditioning professional and self-taught writer.

Dunte competes in masters track & field, travels internationally to meet experts on human performance, and shamelessly promotes his athletes on Instagram @atxspeed. When he is not writing about running faster, he talks about running faster, thinks about running faster, and trains to run faster. You can find him in east Austin with his athletes or with his kids.

Sign up for the Speed & Strength Newsletter for training blog updates and news about upcoming ATX Speed events, projects, and roster openings.

Be sure to leave a review on Amazon for other readers!

69061055R00059

Made in the USA
Lexington, KY
24 October 2017